Navigating the Financial Forest

Personal Economics for Anyone

Dennis Boyd Call

ISBN: 9781090645968
Imprint: Independently published

DEDICATION

Dedicated to my late wife, Connie, who held things together in the tough times and guided us wisely in the good times.

CONTENTS

ACKNOWLEDGMENTS

I acknowledge my children, Camielle, Bruce, Denalee, Michael, Jennilyn and Darryn. Without them, I would have missed out on many of life's lessons, including many important lessons related to personal and family finance.

THE FINANCIAL FOREST

I recently searched on-line for books on personal finance. It was an interesting adventure. What I found were a plethora of books on becoming wealthy, avoiding taxes, filing for bankruptcy and investing strategies. There was a bit of information on how to manage personal or family finances, but I found much of it rather void of practical advice. As a result, I have decided to write this little Quick-Read book in the hope that it might give assistance to someone in need of help, but who does not know where to find it.

Perhaps the dearth of available informative books is because those who could write one feel that those who need it cannot afford to buy it. The problem with that thinking is this: My experience indicates almost everyone can afford it. They just need some advice on how to free up the money to purchase it; or worse yet, they feel that there is no way that they can ever get out of their financial hole and so … what's the use?

My credentials for writing this Quick-Read book include having been well-off and having been poor; *well-off is better*. It would have been healthier for our family finance if I had applied certain principles of money management earlier in life. But I didn't! Perhaps you can learn from my past errors and current knowledge.

I am an octogenarian with many years of experience as a Financial Advisor. Additionally, I have been self-employed in private construction and a principle in businesses with associates. More privately, I have served as a lay minister wherein I spent many hours counseling with folks who "could not make ends meet."

While I would not wish extremely difficult financial times upon anyone, I am grateful for the many things I learned during my own times of financial trial. They were excruciatingly painful, educational and eye-opening!

Inside of these covers you will find personal experiences; some of my own and some of others. These experiences involved not only the handling of personal finances but the horrifying effects that money problems could have on health, marriage and reputation. You will read about dealing with family demands, creditor demands and conscience demands.

There will probably be some who read this book who feel that I give a bit of Voodoo advice. That is okay. Please though, just remember that this writing comes from my personal, business and ecclesiastical experiences.

Many years ago, I was invited as a professional advisor into someone's home to evaluate their circumstance and make some financial recommendations. I was a bit perplexed because as our phone conversation progressed, I learned that the husband was in a profession that compensated him deeply into a six-figure income and the wife was involved as a part owner in a small specialty business. They lived in a "dream" community, a highly regarded area of wealth and prominence. It would seem that they were well placed socially and financially.

As I entered their home I was first directed into a portion of the home that held some very valuable collectibles. The items were clearly their pride and joy; they proudly described the rarity and cost of each treasure. They surely must have seen a perplexed look on my face because they quickly said something like, *"The investment value of these pieces is immense."* Given what the items consisted of, I was certain of the truth of that statement.

We next went into the kitchen to have our meeting around the family table. In doing so, we proceeded through the living room which contained no furniture save a couple of hardback chairs. They stated, *"We haven't gotten around to furnishing the living room yet."* The extended situation, as I later learned, was that they had precious little furniture in any room. They had a late model luxury automobile in their garage and another one in the driveway. From all outward appearance, they were truly living the American dream.

This couple had a problem that existed because they were maintaining their lifestyle through the extensive use of their very high limit credit cards. I am not sure what they expected of me as an advisor/counselor but they did not find it. Early in the conversation it became clear that they were not willing to give up anything that would put a damper on their standard of living. They were just unable to make the "sacrifice." I did not take them on as clients.

I ultimately made the decision to focus my business on a segment of the population that might be more receptive to some painful paradigm shifts. Does that mean that everyone quickly embraced my analyses and recommendations? Unfortunately no, not everyone; but there were enough who appreciated my assistance that it kept me on the track; I kept on *keepin' on.*

In the chapters that follow, I will share stories of some very successful financial turn-arounds, as well as some that were unsuccessful because of pride, vanity and self-absorption.

Stories are wonderful means of teaching and learning; but there is much more to it. These chapters will include discussions on interest rates, credit card usage, mortgages and unexpected financial downturns.

Education can be like the falling tree in the forest
It matters only if someone hears and learns
Especially true in personal finance

LOST IN THE FOREST

Have you ever been lost … anywhere? Being truly lost means that you not only don't know where you are, but that you do not even know what direction to go. You do not know how far away the nearest sign of civilization may be, and so you just wander in the hope that somewhere, somehow it will all work out. You do the best that you can. Being lost in the Financial Forest can be a similar experience.

Having a financial GPS could help, but that by itself would only tell you what direction, how far and how much time it will take to get you to your destination. *"So what's the problem?"* You ask. *"We are on our way out!"*

Well, the problem is that you still have to make the effort, take the time and work around the inherent problems. Thus, in doing so you will find financial scrub-brush, rainstorms and wild boars to impede your efforts. One scary thing about wild boars is that they are nocturnal animals that forage for food at night while you are trying to get some peaceful sleep! As a result, while getting out of your financial predicament is desirable, possible and important, it can be intimidating and scary. A sort of paralytic fear can set in.

Your brain is filled with imaginary gremlins running around helter-skelter, bumping into each other and creating chaos; so much so that you cannot seem to get rational in your pursuit of financial sanity. Other obstacles loom larger than life. You feel as though you will never be found; suddenly not only are you lost in the Financial Forest, but you discover that you are actually on an island without a boat and you cannot swim!

Ridiculous metaphor? Perhaps, but this is a good place to share a true-life experience. A lady, Mary, who seemed to have everything life has to offer came to see me. Her husband of many years was suddenly taken from her. Yesterday he was here, today he is gone! The suddenness of the situation would cause great consternation in anyone's mind and Mary's situation was just that: Anxiety, worry and complete befuddlement!

The portion of her state of affairs that I was consulted on was of course, her financial well-being. Mary had only a cursory knowledge of their family finances. She knew Tom had a 401k at work and she was able to retrieve a statement. Her knowledge of bank balances, indebtedness and the status of monthly bills was miniscule. *"Tom always took care of that and I didn't need to worry about it,"* was her explanation.

Soon Mary's mind had begun to think about her life in the future without Tom. It would be lonely she knew, but how am I going to pay for things, *"You know, like the house payment, the power bill and all of that?"* All she began see were the scrub-brush, the rainstorms and the wild boars on the island she was lost in. She knew basically nothing about their financial condition. Their three children were grown and beginning their own families. They had no knowledge of Dad and Mom's finances, nor were they in a financial situation to assist Mom if she needed it. Mary was lost among countless others in the Financial Forest; not uncommon!

I have learned that Mary's situation typifies one of the most egregious mistakes that can take place in a home; only one spouse handles the all finances. In some cases that spouse takes advantage. In some cases the "financial" spouse may make an unintentional error that handicaps the family's ability to pay the bills. The solution? Both spouses should be engaged in the family finances. They should discuss the bills, the prioritization of payments, the shortfalls and the windfalls.

My own record of doing these things was pretty dismal in our early years of marriage. Too many times I encumbered our family with new car purchases: there was no discussion or approval. I just expected acceptance by Connie. Fortunately, she was very forgiving; and thankfully I was not taken away during those years. Had my life been taken, she would definitely have been lost in the Financial Forest, all alone … except for the six children she would have been called upon to raise by herself.

It was following a number of years of the, *"Surprise, Honey, guess what I have for you!"* existence that my wife insisted on a heart-to-heart talk. It was then that I opened up about our finances. She still wanted me to pay the bills; she just insisted that she be "in the know," good, bad or indifferent.

Having both spouses "in the know" will not always eliminate the financial crisis; it is a rather common occurrence. But with both spouses being aware of the family finances, the weight of a downturn is greatly mitigated. Sometimes there is an employment change that downgrades the income. There may be an unexpected medical expense, or the need for a new refrigerator when the budget is already stretched to the limit.

None of us is exempt from the possibilities, but most of us will benefit if there is open dialogue between both heads of the family.

Marriage itself is a partnership; thus, family finance is a shared responsibility. I have known husbands who have declared, *"I earn the family income; I will decide how to spend it!"* Very short-sighted, in my opinion.

Many of the "lost in the Financial Forest" happenings can be avoided; but many of them are unavoidable. A great many of them can be avoided if one has a clear understanding of very basic principles. Two of those principles are: Plan for the unexpected and Prepare for what you planned.

In the planning phase, there are two definite values that should be assumed will happen. **1)** An emergency will arise and **2)** Someday we will want to retire. *Both will require money!*

The first: The emergency is a surprise visit by the unknown or at least the unexpected. A certain amount of savings must be built into the monthly budget; it is simply an emergency fund that you feed money into from every paycheck. It does not need to be a large amount every payday but it should be consistent.

The second: Retirement is usually not a surprise. It is a long-term objective that also needs to be fed. I have occasionally been asked, *"How much money will I need for retirement?"* I have a very firm opinion on this, *"It depends."*

It depends upon your lifestyle, where you live in retirement and how much traveling you anticipate; just to name three things out of a multitude. In a subsequent chapter, retirement will be further discussed.

> ***It is one thing to plan***
> ***It is another thing to act***
> ***It takes both to prepare***

I HEARD ABOUT A BUDGET ONCE, UGH!

Budget: An estimate of income and expenditure for a set period of time ... The amount of money needed or available for a purpose. (Oxford Dictionary)

Budget: The amount of money that is available for, required for, or assigned to a particular purpose (Merriam-Webster Dictionary)

I have met very few people who operate their family finances on a strict budget, or on *any* budget for that matter. They see a budget as being too restrictive and limiting. It is true that many people do live within their income, have no financial problems and are getting along just fine. If this describes you, the ideas in this book may very well enhance your financial niceties.

Understanding, creating and living within a budget sometimes takes uncomfortable effort and dedication. Besides, no one cares for restrictions; self-imposed or otherwise. Personal budgets fall somewhere in the terrible categories of diets and alarm clocks. Besides, we all know that our government officials while they *do* create a national budget every year, cannot seem to operate the country within their self-created constraints; so why should we bother to live within our own personal budgets?

Additionally, money is there to be spent … is it not? After all, we are helping the economy by circulating our currency … aren't we? Sometimes little thought seems to be given to the source of our money; government or personal.

Unfortunately, we who are in the ranks of normal citizenry must earn money the old-fashioned way: With our heart, hands and head. Therefore, it behooves us to be prudent with our spending. The equation is quite simple: Spend less than you earn! As I have looked at, analyzed and tried to make sense of the bank statements and credit card bills of many people, I find a very common theme: Those in financial trouble cannot, or will not reconcile spending against income. This is where a personal or family budget becomes a very valuable and essential tool.

Prior to creating a budget, it is important for one to identify his current spending pattern. Without this, the person will see little need for a formal budget. In order to learn about spending patterns, you should analyze your three most current bank statements. Just reviewing one's own cash outflow is occasionally sufficient; but, some people still don't get it. If this is you, a massive educational course becomes significant. The imperative thing in understanding and creating your budget is that you must be brutally honest in assessing your current spending habits.

The reality can be stark and somewhat frightening when a person realizes the amount of money he (or she) spends on soda pop, candy and snacks. However, food spending is not the only infraction that can be found through the close examination of monthly bank statements. There are excessive purchases at personal care shops, handyman do-dads and "last-chance" internet offers that are just too appealing to ignore … and so we don't. It is the excess that we are looking for, not the necessities. But the necessities must be included when putting your budget together.

The companion piece to your bank statements is a daily cash accounting worksheet. Prior to asking any of my clients to use one, I practiced on myself for many months. I was amazed at the revelation unfolding before me as I saw the incredible amount of soda pop I was drinking. I already knew that I spent a lot of "loose" money, but what it was spent on was incredibly stunning! The impact on my common sense and the educational shock that I experienced convinced me that others could also benefit from what I had learned; so I put it into practice with clients.

One couple who came to me because, *"We just cannot make ends meet"* had a significant unplanned-for benefit. Both of these delightful people were somewhat overweight and they stated that they wanted to join a gym but couldn't afford it.

They entered into a three-month plan and committed to follow it through to completion. Not only did they discover gross reckless use of their debit card, they virtually eliminated their wasteful spending. By stopping their adverse eating habits, they each lost a significant amount of weight. In fact, at the end of three months, they came into my office full of smiles and announced to me, *"Mike is wearing our eighteen-year-old son's jeans!"* I don't know just what size he had been wearing previously, but he was now wearing thirty-two inch pants. They were both looking fit and very trim.

On the following page is an image of a daily cash accounting worksheet. I encourage you to create one for yourself. In order to make this system effective, begin immediately! Withdraw an amount of cash from the bank that is equal to your anticipated cash needs until the next paycheck. Cash needs are those expenditures of less than twenty dollars. Write that amount in the top left cell of the spreadsheet; this equals the *total* amount of cash you will carry with you and will be your *only* source of "spending" money.

Enter each day's cash expenditures in the appropriate cell across the sheet and subtract it from the beginning balance. Do this exercise for at least ninety days. DO NOT CHEAT! Verify *each day* that your remaining cash is exactly equal to the amount shown in the "balance" column. It will help if you obtain a receipt for *every* purchase. Vending machine buys will require immediate recording. Calculate to the very penny. Again, DO NOT CHEAT! If you can re-create this spreadsheet on your computer, do so.

Daily Cash Accounting Month:			Name:					Make entries Every Day!
Day	Begin Cash	Pop	Candy	Lunch	Snacks	Personal Care	Other (Identify)	Balance Cash
1								$0.00
2								$0.00
3								$0.00
4								$0.00
5								$0.00
6								$0.00
7								$0.00
8								$0.00
9								$0.00
10								$0.00
11								$0.00
12								$0.00
13								$0.00
14								$0.00
15								$0.00
16								$0.00
17								$0.00
18								$0.00
19								$0.00
20								$0.00
21								$0.00
22								$0.00
23								$0.00
24								$0.00
25								$0.00
26								$0.00
27								$0.00
28								$0.00
29								$0.00
30								$0.00
31								$0.00
Totals:	0.00	0.00	0.00	0.00	0.00	0.00		

A serious and sometimes brutal look at just one months' results should be sufficient to generate a major adjustment. Keeping it going for three months will make you feel wonderful because you can see your progress almost on a daily basis. As you feel the cash leaving your pocket, you should feel an equalizing sense of caution regarding future spending. Do not wait for three months to begin the next step: Simultaneously, begin generating your budget.

There are four categories of personal expenses. **1) Fixed** necessary expenses, **2) Variable** necessary expenses, **3) Important** expenses but not crucial to your existence, **4) Nice** expenses, but only if the surplus will permit. Categories 3) and 4) are shelf items; shelf items are those things which are not necessary to sustain life.

Some people simplify the process by classifying them as **1) Needs** and **2) Wants**. This is fine, however it is not always easy to distinguish one from the other. I prefer the four-category approach. Either way, every expense that you have must be accounted for. Be aware: This is what causes many people to give up and accept their plight.

I recommend that the following process be used in the physical creation of a budget. It can be done concurrent with the three-month evaluation of one's current spending pattern. (There is no good reason to take any longer than necessary to prepare your budget; it just prolongs the pain.)

The steps are simple and I do not intend to be condescending to anyone. However, since many people get caught up in the minutia of numbers when they begin this first step, I want to help ease the paralytic inertia that can easily be the result. So that being said, let's begin with a four-column ledger sheet. *Do not even think about numbers as you begin the process!* Numbers at this point will only serve to obfuscate the thought process.

Label each column from left to right in these four categories: **1) Fixed 2) Variable 3) Important 4) Nice.** Then identify the proper expenses in the column beneath the appropriate heading. *This page is for identification purposes only.* Use the following short list as a guide to get started.

1) Fixed: Tithe or ten percent to charity, Ten percent to yourself, Rent/house payment, utilities, etc.

2) Variable: Groceries, phone etc.,

3) Important: Manicure, barber etc.,

4) Nice: Cruise, vacation trip etc.

Columns three and four are "shelf" items and will be considered when we know that there is sufficient money available each month.

Now take a second sheet of paper with five columns. Identify the five columns in this manner: **1) Income 2) Expense items 3) Expense budget 4) Expense actual 5) Difference**.

The first column: In this column, identify every source of income using its monthly value. Here is where some people get confused. If one gets paid one time per month, it is easy: twelve paychecks per year. If one gets paid on the first and the fifteenth it is still easy because adding the two paydays together gives the total monthly income; twenty-four paychecks per year.

If one gets paid every two weeks, the math is a little more tricky because there are now twenty-six paychecks in the year. Annualize your income by multiplying the amount of a single paycheck by twenty-six, then divide the total by twelve. The result is your monthly income.

Regardless of which pay schedule you are on, write the monthly amount in the first column under "income."

The second column: Here is where you begin to copy from page one. Copy every *Fixed* expense item in this column. Following the Fixed items and in the same column, copy in the *Variable* expense items from page one. At this point stop inserting expense items.

The third column: Here is where you will start with the numbers. This is also where your bank statements will come in handy, or your monthly billing statement or perhaps you have your fixed expenses memorized. Whatever the source, fill in the amount of money that you expend on each fixed items listed in column two.

Following the fixed expenses, write the variable expense amount. I recommend that the annual average (or at least three months average) amount be used. (Obtained from your bank statements.)

Total each column at the bottom. (Income column then the expense column.) Subtract the total expense amount from the income amount. That is the amount available for the Important and the Nice items. Simple, right? Nope, not so quick; do not itemize any shelf items until you have experienced a minimum of one month and preferable three months of actual expenditures.

The fourth column: This column is not activated until you have paid your monthly bill. As you pay each of your fixed and variable expenses, write that amount in column four. Some of these monies (groceries for example) are expended multiple times during the month. It will be necessary to keep receipts or a separate accounting every time money is spent, then added as a whole at the end of the month on your budget sheet, in this column. When each line item is paid, you will start to utilize column five.

The fifth column: Subtract every line item in column four from column three and write the difference in this column. Each of your *fixed* expenses should have a zero difference here. Hopefully, your variable actual expenses will be less than the planned, or budgeted amount; if the difference is zero, that is wonderful. You kept that item within budget.

The variable items may be over or under budget. This is the reason that the shelf items should not be considered until you have proven an appropriate amount for each fixed and variable expenditure. I realize that three months is quite a while for some important items, but if you can pull it off, you will be on the shortcut path out of the Financial Forest.

You have now reached the "rubber meets the road" point of this entire exercise. Subtract column four from column one and place that amount at the bottom of column five. Congratulations! You know the amount of this month's surplus. Put it in your savings account. But heaven forbid that the number is negative. If it is, at least you know what you are dealing with, and you know how deep into the forest you are. You are at the beginning of the path out!

Assuming that you have a positive number, you can then prioritize which item or items to bring off the shelf. You can make them a part of your permanent budget or perhaps, alternate on a monthly basis those items on which you choose to spend your money. *Remember, just because there is money left over does not mean it has to be spent.* Adding the excess to your savings account brings with it a wonderful feeling of success in money management.

If your expenses are greater than your income, you may find it necessary to take a second job, move to a less expensive home or (perish the thought) move in with your parents!

But when that situation does occur, there is never any reason nor right in my opinion, to spend money on any shelf item. I make this statement fully understanding that given my past performance, it is a bit of an incongruity. More than once, in our young years, Connie and I spent our last few dollars on a movie. But do not use this comment as justification for your own continued mis-spending of your money. Remember, you are to benefit from my mistakes.

Traversing through the remaining chapters of this book, we will consider shelf items, impulse items, important surprise items and opportunity items. Emergency items, compassion items and items of *grace* will also be addressed.

It is going to be an enlightening and beneficial ride through the Financial Forest. For many readers there will be totally new concepts and viewpoints. Other readers may find some concepts already known but need to be re-activated.

If you do not manage your money
Your money will manage you
If your money manages you
You have an uncaring taskmaster

TALKING ABOUT MONEY MAKES ME SICK

Money in our society is a fact of life, and until there is a major overhaul of world economies it will remain a fact of life. It is just one of those things that *is*. It is one of those things that we must deal with, as difficult as it happens to sometimes be.

So what must you do that will ease your frustrations, your financial hurts and your emotional distresses? First, it is important to prioritize your priorities. You have needs, I have needs, we all have needs. The difference is that a need for you may not be a need for me; thus there is no absolute need that appears in the same hierarchal order. In 1943, Abraham Maslow introduced his physiological hierarchy of needs as part of his "A Theory of Human Motivation." At the pinnacle of his hierarchy is "Self-actualization: Achieving one's full potential including creative activities." [1]

I believe that having ones' financial affairs under control is one major step in fulfilling Maslow's proposed premier position. But even though we all have needs that may fall within the same category, the prioritization may be different. For example: I am a

---

[1] Maslow, "A Theory of Human Motivation"

self-admitted news junkie so television ranks high in my priorities; yet, I know people who are doing wonderfully well with no TV in their homes.

When I queried a parent in one family about the reason for no TV in their home, I was told, *"In the beginning, we could not afford it. As the family began to expand, and we were spending a lot of time together we realized something. We were reading, talking and playing games together. It was then we learned that it was a benefit to us to have no television; and as a family we have wonderful personal interactions."*

According to surveys the number two reason for divorce in America is linked to finance.[2] That would be lack of, not agreeing on management of, or one partner being in control of, the family finances. There could be many additional reasons but suffice it to say, money does matter! When both husband and wife understand and participate in the creating of a budget, the paying of bills and decisions on major purchases, there is more peace and harmony in the home.

Depression brought about by financial concerns is not uncommon. I know one man who's severe depression over the family's budget disarray led to physical ailments that led to even more expense. He developed serious stomach illness and it was even the cause of his teeth falling out. There are obviously a multitude of practical reasons for creating and maintaining personal and family budgets. But there are other more ethereal reasons for doing so. I call them giving back … some call it paying forward.

Naturally, there are those things that must be at the top of every budget; such as rent or house payment, utilities and food. But there

---

[2] Marriage.com

is one item that should be at first place in every budget. This item is faith-based, and it applies across all faiths. That item is Tithing; ten-percent of your earnings should be paid to the Lord. You do this by contributing to your church, whatever that church may be. The math often does not work out when it is put on paper; however, the Lord's math is frequently different than man's math.

I love telling the story of the young couple who came to my office looking for a path through the Financial Forest. They had recently moved to Texas from another state where they had lost all of their savings in a real estate deal gone bad. Further, his employment position had been eliminated and they were facing financial obliteration. These delightful people had one child and another on the way. Another bright spot was that he did have employment in Texas, but the pay was inadequate for their needs; he was earning fifty-thousand dollars per year.

They provided the requested three months bank statement for my analysis. I asked a number of questions about items in the bank statements which were easily answered; finally I inquired about a consistent forty-dollar per month withdrawal from their bank statement. *"Oh,"* they answered proudly, *"That is our tithing and we pay it every month."*

I was favorably impressed with their faith and diligence, and I replied, *"Wonderful! That is a nice donation, but it is not tithing."* Walking across my office to my desk, I picked up my Bible and returned to the conference table. We turned to the Book of Malachi where the discussion on tithes and offerings takes place. After a brief conversation about tithing and its meaning, they said in near unison, *"We will do it. The Lord promises that He will open the windows of heaven to us and we believe Him."*[3]

---

[3] See Holy Bible, KJV, Malachi 3:8-10

They expressed concern that going from forty-dollars per month to more than four-hundred-dollars every month would create a huge concern. Even so, they made the commitment; I was admittedly very impressed by that pledge.

We spoke several times over the next three months; they were able to make their payments and keep up to date on their bills. Then just three months into their journey of coming out of the forest, they came into my office in a giddy mood and almost bouncing off the walls. So infectious were they that I almost bounced with them. They couldn't wait to sit down before she blurted, *"He got a promotion at work!"*

They explained that with the promotion came a nice raise in salary. *"Really,"* I grinned, *"And how much was the raise?"* Even I was amazed at the answer.

He said, *"Twenty-five-thousand-dollars a year. I got a fifty-percent pay increase!!"*

Somewhat stunned, I asked, *"How in the world did that come about?"*

She looked at me in a mock incredulous stare and replied, *"We paid our tithing, of course! Just as you taught us to do."*

Further discussion revealed that following our first meeting three months prior, they began with full faith. Out of their next semi-monthly paycheck they first paid two-hundred-ten-dollars to their church, and repeated the process each subsequent payday.

Will everyone get such an increase so quickly after beginning to pay their tithing? Probably not, but God has made His promise and He cannot lie. I find no stipulation in Holy scriptures that one must be of any particular faith, denomination or persuasion in order for His promise to work. My suggestion is: No matter how deep into the forest you are, try it because you may like it.

The payment of tithing takes a lot of faith in God. When finances are tight and one must struggle just to keep the lights on, it seems like an impossible promise, even to many who believe in God. My own personal experiences, however, have been sufficient for me to know that regular and consistent payment of tithing works! It benefits me and it benefits others; it is a commandment of God; a win-win-win situation.

I know the feeling of having multiple bill collectors calling on the phone almost every day. Or more distressing to me was having the "wild boars" calling my wife while I was at work. The stress on our marriage was almost palpable but we made it through.

The tactics used by those financial nocturnal animals is beyond the pale and in many cases illegal. They have called outside of the legal hours, made threats and used intimidation all in their attempt to collect whatever they could. It is good to understand how the collection system sometimes work.

The original creditor (the credit card company) after a number of months, has given up on collecting the money you owe. They can use the write-off so they cut their losses and sell your account to a collection service for fifty-cents on the dollar. The collection service is incentivized by the thought that they now have the possibility of doubling their investment. In reality, they must surely know that the chances of doing that is remote; so they feel that making a profit of fifty percent is much more possible.

They then embark on making the phone calls and within a few months of futile contacts, they do as did the original creditor and sell your account for ten-cents on the dollar. It seems to me that the farther away from the original creditor the collection agency is, the more intimidating is their tactic. I suppose it must be effective because many of these companies are still in business, although I understand that laws have been enacted which are intended to rein in the most egregious offenders.

Ultimately, one of these three things usually happens: **1)** You make some sort of repayment arrangements with the agency, and your credit rating reflects the serious delinquencies. **2)** They ultimately give up and leave you alone but your credit rating is totally decimated and it takes years for you to recover financially and emotionally. **3)** You file for bankruptcy and your debts are forgiven, but your credit rating is damaged and the bankruptcy stays on your credit report for ten years.

I have been asked this question: Is it wrong to file for bankruptcy? I give the same answer as I do to other questions, *"I depends."* I think it depends on whether or not you purposely ran up debt. If you did that feeling that filing bankruptcy will clear up the money problems, it is definitely wrong.

On the other hand, if economic disaster strikes and you are caught in the crosshairs of someone else's bad financial actions, I feel that the bankruptcy laws are there to help you. Bankruptcy is not illegal but most people with whom I have worked, feel a serious moral repugnancy against it. But I have seen it work miracles in the lives of many couples. In my opinion, it can be a very difficult personal decision for anyone to face.

No matter how bad off you feel
There is someone in worse condition
Do your best to help those whom you can
Employ the Lord's method and put Him to the test

COMPOUNDING OR CONFOUNDING INTEREST?

My eighth grade math teacher, Melvin Jones was one who did not stop as long as there was a student who needed his help! He used practical real-life happenings that we could relate to as he taught us about such things as algebra and compound interest. Mathematical conundrums were effective teaching tools for him and effective learning tools for me.

Compound interest is one of those facts in the Financial Forest that many people fail to appreciate; it is a major cause of people becoming lost in the forest. The importance of understanding this somewhat dark part of finance cannot be overstated. Albert Einstein said, *"Compound interest is the eighth wonder of the world. He who understands it, earns it ... he who doesn't ... pays it."*[4] In some of Mr. Jones' math classes we explored the magic of the compounding of numbers.

Think of the old riddle, *"Would you rather have me give you ten dollars now, or would you rather I give you one penny today and double the amount every day for a month?"*

---

[4] Quotesonfinance.com

In your short-sightedness, you impulsively agree that it would be best to take the ten dollars. That is often the way people look at major purchases; credit card balances and impulse buying. None of these three methods of spending your money is bad, in-and-of itself. It is the unrestrained use of any, or all three of them that cause grief. Additionally it is the deferred payment methods and the blindness with which we sometimes act, that get us into trouble.

Now back to the puzzle: Let's look at the impact of the choice we made when we opted for the ten dollars rather than the doubling of the penny every day:

1) Ten dollars is just that; ten dollars, but you do get it immediately!

2) One cent today, doubled tomorrow gives you a total of two cents. Doubled the next day (day three) results in a total of four cents … you get the picture: double the total each day and in eleven days you have ten dollars and twenty-four cents; a bit more than the ten dollars you foolishly opted for in the beginning. Carry the formula out for the full 30 days … can you spell multi-millionaire? If you came up with five-million, three-hundred sixty-eight-thousand, seven-hundred nine dollars and twelve cents, you would be correct. That is the amount of the take on the thirtieth day only - you did not add in the base penny and it's compounding effect!

This little foray into the Financial Forest is simply a fun little experiment into compounding at the rate of one-hundred percent per day. Now let's get a bit more realistic. There is a valuable rule of thumb that should be known and understood by everyone. That is the "Rule of Seventy-two."

Easily stated it is to the borrower: If you borrow any amount of money at an interest rate of five percent and you make no payments, your debt will have doubled in approximately fourteen and one-half years. To the saver it means that your deposit of any amount into a Certificate of Deposit paying five-percent, will have doubled in the same fourteen and one-half years. *"So what does seventy-two have to do with it,"* you ask. Well, here is the answer to your question.

The formula is extremely simple but is not exact; further, it works on smaller numbers like you and I use, not on really high finance. Get out your calculator (it is right there on your phone) and do this: Divide any interest rate into the number seventy-two and the resulting answer is the number of years it will take to double your debt (or your deposit).

Now let's get a little more realistic and consider credit card debt. Few people are fortunate enough to carry credit cards with a five-percent interest rate. Most likely the rate is anywhere from twelve-percent to nearly thirty-percent. Let's suppose you owe the credit card company three-thousand dollars; they are charging you eighteen-percent and you make no payments, how long will it take for your debt to become six-thousand dollars? I give that to you as your homework assignment.

"But," you say, *"The credit card company insists that I pay a minimum amount each month so that helps, doesn't it?"* Sure, but remember it is a very minimal amount. For your convenience (and because the law makes them do it) your credit card statement has a little box that shows just how long it will take to pay your debt if you make only minimum payments. But that is only if you do not make any additional purchases with that card. Suddenly an emergency arises! You need a car repair, it goes on your card and you find yourself in a financial tailspin downward into the middle

of the forest! New charges go onto the back end of your debt and increases your minimum payment, your interest and your angst!

In checking with bankrate.com I find that currently, the highest paying eighteen-month Certificate of Deposit (CD) pays a whopping 2.80% Annual Percentage Rate (APR). The highest paying Money Market (MM) pays 2.40% APR.

So let's get this straight. Assume you maintain a consistent two-thousand dollar balance on your credit card; the credit card company charges 18% interest. At the end of eighteen months you will have paid your credit card company a total of five-hundred-forty dollars in interest.

However, if you maintain a two-thousand dollars balance in the MM account that pays you 2.40% interest on your savings, you would have earned seventy-two dollars over the same eighteen months. The question becomes: Which would you rather have happen to you; earn seventy-two dollars or give the bank five-hundred forty dollars? This amounts to a spread of six-hundred-twelve dollars.

If you are paying 28% interest on your card, the net spread amounts to eight-hundred-twelve dollars over the eighteen month period. The net spread being the total amount you would have spent versus the total amount you would have earned … or in a language that may be more visual: You could be eight-hundred-forty feet underground or you could be on top of a seventy-two foot mound of earth.

You may be correct in saying that the percentage difference between paying interest and earning interest is unfair. That is not what this discourse is about. This treatise is about getting out of, and staying away from wandering aimlessly in the Financial

Forest. In short: Do not go into debt for unnecessary, senseless or superfluous things!

You must weigh the cost of purchasing anything against the benefit of having it. This is especially true when buying on time, be it credit card time or consumer debt contract. Is it really worth the expense?

Several years ago a young couple who were expecting their first child approached me for some advice. They were having a difficult time making ends meet and wanted my input. After looking over three months of bank statements, I asked a question. *"What is the purpose of the six-hundred dollars per month that is extracted from your bank account every month?"*

"Oh, that is our boat payment. We use it every weekend," was the reply. *"You should see it,"* she continued with enthusiasm. *"It is parked in our driveway and we go out on the lake every chance we get."*

I continued, *"What interest rate you are paying for your boat loan? Plus you have insurance, fuel and maintenance costs, right?* The interest rate question was met with a blank stare and the other question was answered in the affirmative.

After a short pause, she asked, *"Well, Dennis, what do you think? Can you help us?"*

"I can," I began. *"I see few items that are non-essential and I suggest that eliminate them. But that will not do much to improve your situation. Therefore, you should sell the boat immediately."*

In stunned disbelief, I was informed that they could not do that. They needed the boat because it was their escape. It was an impossible suggestion. The boat had become their God; it was almost a worshipful adulation that they held for it.

They had no clue as to the real cost of owning their boat. I suspect that without some major reformation in their standard of living, they probably gave the boat up to repossession. They did agree to a follow-up meeting but failed to attend. Were they lost in the Financial Forest? Most definitely!

In 1969 we moved from Southern California to Michigan and there we purchased a new home. The banker that we dealt with for our mortgage allowed us a mortgage rate of seven percent. He said, *"This is the last seven percent mortgage we will write. You will never see that low of a rate again."*

Over the following years I thought of his statement; ten years after his remark, I marveled in my mind about the prophetic nature of his comment. Inflation and interest rates soared into double digits and anyone with a seven percent mortgage was greatly envied. The rates remained above that seven percent benchmark for many years. It was in about 2008 that rates descended rapidly to below four percent and many people rushed to re-finance their homes.

Was that a good move for them to make? In most cases, I believe it was. When would it not have been wise? Well, if a couple had their higher-rate mortgage almost paid off, they were getting ready to retire, the mortgage company charged an unreasonably high origination fee and they committed to another thirty (or even fifteen) year mortgage, I would question their judgement.

Being lost is one thing
Refusing to be found is another

WILL THAT BE CREDIT OR DEBIT?

I once heard a customer say when asked how he planned to pay for a purchase in a store, *"Oh, I will use plastic; that beats paying for it."* He then proceeded to put the charge on his debit card. He had purposely given a jesting response, but it seems to be true in the minds of many people, especially when using a debit card. During the third review of one of my clients' difficult circumstance, the above attitude became true to life to me.

My client and I were working to overcome what I call her "debit-card-addiction." We had reviewed her bank statements over an extended period of time. Her debit card usage was excessive and we had begun her "rehab" plan. After nearly five months of following the plan, her monthly debit card use had declined significantly. She then told me this story:

"When we started on this plan, I was skeptical and didn't feel it necessary. Then one day my debit card was declined for a four dollar purchase. With a stark realization that my bank account was depleted, I hurriedly went home, gathered up some recent purchases and returned them to the store for refunds. Since I had used the debit card to make the purchase, the refund was electronically returned to my bank account.

"That is what it took for me to realize that I had a serious problem!" Seems that the first gentleman's humorous statement had played out: *"Using plastic beats paying for it."*

The plan that my client used was the plan that I discussed in the earlier chapter on budgets. She committed to withdraw an amount from her bank account each payday. The amount withdrawn would be sufficient to pay for with cash, every anticipated purchase of less than twenty dollars. She was to then leave her debit card at home. When she would see and feel the depletion of her pocket cash, she should begin to realize that multiple small purchases can have gigantic results.

The importance of understanding the impact of using plastic instead of cash is increasing. It becomes more and more important because we are gradually moving toward a cashless society. The proponents of this method speak of the efficiency and safety of such a system; I will not argue with that, although I am a bit of a skeptic. The fact is, if we do not become educated about compound interest, debit-card-addiction and how to avoid being lost in the Financial Forest, we will see the day of financial subjugation enter permanently into our lives.

To those who are already lost and wandering in the Financial Forest, you are experiencing a portion of that subjugation now.

The simple swipe of the card certainly is convenient and in many cases there is no pain felt. After all, it is only one dollar and ninety-eighty cents. In my case referred to earlier, it was a shocker for me to come face-to-face with the fact that I was spending between seventy-five and one-hundred dollars a month on soda pop! And I was not even using a debit card. I just knew I was spending a lot of cash and the daily accounting worksheet made me understand very clearly where my money was going. It was a tough awakening!

So, what to do? For starters, use plastic very sparingly, debit and credit. And while it may be difficult to exist in our society without one or the other (or both) they do not need to be used constantly. I suggest that you put yourself on a cash, check or on-line bill pay system except for the paycheck-to-paycheck cash withdrawal program you are now using.

If you do need to use your debit card, enter the amount of your purchase *every day* into your check register. Deduct that amount from your bank account balance promptly. By doing this, you will be paying attention to the fact that your bank account balance is being reduced!

Reconcile your bank statement every month. It is not difficult; Mr. Jones taught us eighth graders how to do it, so I know you can do it. The bank statements that I am familiar with even include a form and instructions for doing so.

While much less subtle but equally onerous and almost always much more expensive is uncontrolled credit card use. To illustrate my point I will tell another story involving a family who came to me with severe problems. Their marriage was disintegrating and his attitude was one of despair, and he was close to giving up completely. She was aware of their financial plight but chose to be oblivious to the extreme toll it was taking on their marriage.

These otherwise delightful people were tens of thousands in debt to various credit card companies. Yet they maintained a fairly high credit score with the rating companies; they never missed a payment and they were proud of that fact.

I questioned them as to how they had garnered such a large amount of "plastic" debt; debt that was costing them twenty-eight percent interest. Their answer seemed like a no-brainer to them and even gave the impression that I was dumb to even ask the question. They replied, *"When we get close to reaching our credit limit on a card, we take out a new card that gives us several months with no interest. That way we are getting interest-free money."*

I contemplated what I had heard and congratulated them on their astuteness. I commented, *"I suspect that you then continue to use your old card plus any new credit available on your new card. The cycle begins all over again. Am I correct?"* Their heads dropped as they realized just what they had been doing to themselves for several years.

As they left my office he held onto me as his wife walked ahead. This humbled man quietly said to me, *"Do you believe in angels?"* I replied in the affirmative.

He looked at me with teary eyes and said, *"You are my angel."*

Just as this couple had discovered, we many times become financially delusional. We do this to ourselves because we refuse to accept the facts. The facts cause discomfort, guilt and inconvenience; we do not like that!

The plastic card is valuable
The plastic card can be sneaky
The plastic card is not your master
The plastic card has addictive powers

HONEY, I LOST MY JOB TODAY

Very few things can be more disconcerting and disheartening as to show up for work one day just to find that your job has been eliminated. Sometimes these situations can be anticipated and sometimes they are fully unexpected.

There are those times that the job is taken away unexpectedly for other reasons. A sudden health situation is a classic example. Let me share my own experience in this regard. I was fifty-six years of age at the time. I had been with my current employer for just barely eleven years.

I had begun working with this company after my own business of many years failed; I began my new job as a sales representative. Sales and I were made for each other; I was confident and successful in my new career. On a very cold winter morning as Connie and I were on a cross-country trip, I awoke in our hotel room with a horrible headache.

It didn't take long for the medical people to determine that I had suffered a spontaneous brain hemorrhage. I was unable to return to work at my current job. In fact, it was not possible for me to go to work of any sort for several months, and then only part-time.

We were forced into taking early retirement at age fifty-six. To say that we were totally unprepared for such a happening would be an understatement. A little more than a year following the episode, I was well enough to serve voluntarily as a missionary for our church, which we did for three years.

Here is our financial situation at the time: I was too young to qualify for Social Security; but I did qualify for a small pension from my employer. When I say small, I mean a few hundred dollars per month. Fortunately, we had been putting money into my 401k plan at work. With only eleven years into the plan, there was not a huge accumulation of retirement funds available. We had to sell our comfortable home and put our belongings into storage.

We were able to live frugally but comfortably for the next three and one-half years on my pension and income from my retirement plan. Not easy, However, we did it. This allowed me to enter into the financial services business five years after that cold winter morning in western Nebraska. We were starting at scratch, again! But this time at age sixty-one.

I tell this story only to demonstrate my own knowledge of financial distress, and hold empathy for those who go through it. Even when things look bleak, and the forest is overwhelmingly dense with a lot of wild boars and underbrush, there is hope! And there is a way out of the grasp of financial ruin and despair.

I know a man who was dismissed from his job via fax notice! While the dismissal was not unexpected and he was actually relieved, it took a bit of adjustment to accept the cold manner of the act. He had no resources to fall back on but he doubled down on finding new employment. The new job matched his ethics and work skills much better. In retrospect, he claims that he is very glad that the dismissal occurred when it did.

There are multitudes of reasons for the sudden employment displacement. The fact is that it happens. Another fact is that many people are totally unprepared for such a happening. One of the purposes for this book, and particularly this chapter is to help people deal with the suddenness of unemployment.

If unemployment hits your home, what will you do? I suspect that most of you will answer, *"I will find another job."* That is as it should be. In the meantime and while you are between jobs, do you have a cash reserve to fall back onto? Are you willing to take a temporary job during the transition? Do you keep your resume up to date?

Most financial advisors that I know recommend that a family accumulate cash in the amount of six months' expenses. Certainly this takes time and will not be done overnight; but it needs to begin somewhere. Remember in the budget chapter about paying yourself? This is the first reason for doing so. It is the reason why paying yourself should be item number two in your expense priorities.

My suggestion is that you place as much money as possible, even exceeding ten percent, into your savings account until you have reached enough to fund three months' bills. After that, you can ease up a bit; but continue to fund it at ten percent until you have six months' bills covered. Remember, this is cash-need money. From that point forward, your purpose in savings can become investment money, if so desired.

This cash-need money is in addition to your retirement plan at work. If you cannot afford to fund both cash-need and retirement plan money simultaneously, you have a serious decision to make. If all of your savings money goes into your retirement plan and you lose your job, that money can probably be made available to you: HOWEVER, generally speaking, if you are under the age of fifty-nine and one-half, you will pay a penalty to the IRS for early withdrawal. That penalty amounts to ten-percent of your withdrawal. On the other hand, it is nice to see your retirement plan balance start, and increase as early in life as possible. Weigh very carefully your options and make an informed decision as to how you will cover your emergency funding.

I personally suggest that you fully fund the emergency account first; it provides peace of mind, a feeling of security and joy in life. The savings account will not pay you a high interest rate, but that is not its purpose; the purpose is to have immediate cash available in case of emergency.

Once you have fully satisfied your emergency cash reserve, your next priority should be your participation in your employer's retirement plan. That is most commonly a 401k plan, but non-profits, municipalities, educational and federal government organizations have separate, but very similar plans. In most plans, the employer will contribute a matching portion to your contribution. It is *free* money to you! Take advantage of it, and have your contribution be at least as much as they will match.

For the self-employed all of this can become a monumental dilemma. I know, I have been self-employed most of my life. It takes grit, determination and self-discipline to accumulate a cash reserve in any amount. But you can do it!

Regarding money:
To save is to have security
To have security is to have peace
To have peace is to have enjoyment

DON'T TOUCH MY 401K

I have said it myself, I have heard other advisors say it and I have watched as clients suck in their breath when it is mentioned. *"Your 401k investment is sacred money! It is your retirement!"* These are true statements and any intrusion into these funds must be done with a great deal of thought, a very valid reason and a plan to replace it within a short span of time. Let me paint a couple of scenarios for you and then try to reason out a solution.

Scenario one: You have been paying into your 401k plan for several years; it has grown substantially. At the same time, and through excessive use of a high-limit credit card you find yourself stretched to the max and you realize that your interest rate is eating your finances alive. You do the practical thing; you respond to an offer to refinance your credit card debt to a "no interest for a year" offer. The offer? Another credit card with a much higher credit limit. Hmm, sounds like my client in a previous chapter …

Your new card may have come with a higher limit, but you are smarter than the credit card company. The offer to add new debt to your new card is not even tempting; after all, your transferred balance is interest free for twelve months and the minimum payment is easy enough to handle with comfort.

Besides, your old credit card now has a zero balance and you can use that card … until it is again maxed out. You are forced to use your new card … until it too is maxed out; the cycle restarts. Your combined balances amount to about fifteen-thousand dollars.

Scenario two: Your 401k balance is in good shape. You have contributed to it for several years and you are quite comfortable with your ability to sock it away. Suddenly your are hit with a major car repair, but not a problem; you can finance it with your credit card over a few months. You do well in paying down the balance for three months then … you guessed it, another calamity!

You have been using all of your surplus income to pay off the car repair bill and then the hot water heater goes out, and your heating and air conditioning system fails. You have only one way to pay for repairs, your credit card! And so that is what you do. It doesn't take long for you to realize that eighteen percent interest amounts to a lot of money when you owe the fifteen-thousand dollars.

Do these scenarios exist in real-life or did I simply make them up? I will tell you that similar things have happened in the lives of people who have come to me for counsel.

In a case similar to scenario one, the thought was presented for my approval that they borrow enough money from their 401k plan to pay off the credit cards. I asked if they could stop using their cards completely; after a short pause I was informed that it would be very difficult. Their daughter's needs for school clothes and hair stylist would make it virtually impossible. When I suggested that they could shop for clothing at less expensive stores than they had been using, the lady said, *"What? You want me to buy her clothes at Goodwill?"* Needless to say, I advised them that to borrow from their retirement plan was not a good idea until they were prepared to make major adjustments to their lifestyle.

In scenario two, the idea to borrow fifteen-thousand dollars from their 401k was a good idea. They could borrow the money at five percent interest and pay it back over a few years; the interest would be paid back to themselves via the 401k. So in essence, they stopped paying eighteen-percent to the credit card company and started paying five-percent interest to themselves; a net spread of twenty-three-percent to their favor.

These folks had a good grasp on their situation and understood the math. They also had the self-discipline to manage the repay of the amount borrowed.

In my opinion there are often times very valid reasons for invading a 401k plan. But it must be done with a good purpose, a solid plan and a payoff in sight.

Before taking money from your 401k plan, it is vital to understand some how things work. First of all a loan is not always possible. The plan document will set you know if a loan is possible or not. Plans usually allow for hardship withdrawals but it can come at a cost. Remember that you put money into the plan prior to your income tax being withheld from your paycheck.

This means that if you withdraw money (as opposed to borrowing money) you will be subject to paying income taxes on every penny that you withdraw. Additionally, if you are younger than age fifty-nine and one-half you will be subject to an IRS penalty of ten percent of the amount withdrawn.

Now for my disclaimer: Before taking any funds, for any reason, in any amount, discuss the idea with your tax advisor. He understands your income tax situation and can advise you appropriately for your particular situation.

It is important to plan for your retirement and it is also falling more and more on you to do it yourself. By making this statement, I point your mind to the fact that fewer and fewer companies are offering pensions to long-time employees. Instead they are leaving it up to you to fend for yourself and as a result, there is a need for serious retirement planning.

Under today's scenarios and circumstances, your 401k (or similar plan) will be your primary source of retirement income. The second source will probably be Social Security, assuming it will still be available when you reach retirement age.

It is also imperative that you understand the rules under which Social Security operates. That government departments' website, ssa.gov is a good source for much information. Most financial advisors are versed in how the program functions.

Borrow only with a purpose
Borrow only with a plan in place
Borrow only with the discipline to pay it off

AFTER ALL, IT'S JUST MONEY

There are a number of personal finance axioms, principles, and old wives' tales that we should toss into this book someplace, so I will do it here. Some are obvious, some are near impossible and others are *"Uhh, I dunno about that."* I list them here in no particular order:

1) **Spend less than you earn.** This has been covered in one fashion or another in several of the previous chapters and needn't be rehashed here … except! If you are one who's budget is filled with excess wants and nice-to-haves that are causing budget distress, your objective should be to reduce your spending. Eliminate the self-inflicted sores that cause the hurt.

2) **Earn more than you spend.** *"Wait a minute,"* you think. *"Isn't that the same as the first rule?"* Well, yes and no. There are times in the lives of many people when they are frugal and efficient with their money. They spend money only on their needs. Yet, they simply do not make enough money to make ends meet. It that case, the solution to the problem is most likely to take a second job. There is no shame in doing so and it takes away a lot of pressure!

3) **Pay the Lord first.** I have already expounded on this and do not have a lot further to say. Just try it; you may like it.

4) **Pay yourself second.** This can be an exercise in learning self-discipline for some. For others it can be relatively easy but the savings balance seems to grow excessively slowly. And for a third group it is easy and the balance quickly grows into a five-figure, or even a six-figure balance. The fact of the matter is that you absolutely need to have a cash reserve, an emergency fund or what some call a rainy-day fund.

5) **Be careful with impulse buying.** Shop for what you need, and need what you shop for. Earlier, I described an episode that a client of mine experienced through excess usage of her debit card. Out-of-control impulse buying, although different, has similarities to the debit-card addiction. Online offers are often wonderful opportunities. When the offer is something you are shopping for, something you are in need of or something you can afford, go for it! I know people who are what I call "fun-to-have shoppers." You are the ones who should set a limit to your "impulse budget." *In other words: If you need or want it, and you have the uncommitted money to pay for it, go ahead and buy it.*

6) **Pay your fixed expenses third.** Fixed expenses must be paid. Serious penalties are often attached if not paid on time, or at least within a given period of time after the due date. The landlord deserves to be paid and the utility companies are within their rights to cut off your electricity or water if they are not paid.

7) **Know the difference between necessities and wants.** I have heard it said that sometimes we live with a want for so long that it becomes a necessity. Perhaps the television

service plan you signed up for is overloaded with features that are rarely used or your cellphone plan carries more expense than necessary. I know one family that compared auto insurance rates and changed companies because the savings was in excess of one-hundred dollars per month. The insurance is a necessity, but not all providers are alike.

8) **Utilize a budget.** What can I say that I have not already said? Only this: If you are having month left over at the end of your money, you need a budget! If you do not have a clue where your money is spent, you need a budget! And you need to stick with it and to it.

9) **Reconcile your bank account every month.** It would be interesting to know just how many people actually reconcile their personal accounts regularly. Most of the clients with whom I have worked do not do so, in fact many do not have a clue as to how to do it. Besides, why is it so darned important? Well, for one thing, it helps to manage your budget when you can verify where your money is being spent. For another thing, it gives you control and power over your own finances. Otherwise, you are functioning under the record keeping, the integrity of, and thus the control of, your bank. Rarely have I ever found a mistake by the bank, but I *have* found a few through the process of reconciling my accounts.

10) **Don't spend your money paying for dead horses**. In other words: Pay your credit card bills in full every month. I suspect that to a huge part of our population, this is the impossible dream. However it can be done and the feeling of freedom can be immense. In managing personal finances, the weight of ongoing interest charges can be so burdensome that one's entire life can be negatively affected. When you get behind in payments, the collectors

become incessant, blatant and sometimes threatening to deal with.

11) **Do not fall for get-rich-quick schemes.** They do not work and when something seems too good to be true, it probably is. There are scams right and left, they are in emails, on telephones, instant messaging and text. They come in the form of blackmail, IRS threats, Social Security threats, and offers of millions of dollars just for a small courier fee. The United States Postal Service deals with the fallout of these scams to the amount of millions of dollars every year.

Legitimate company logos, verbiage and appearances are used and can be very official looking. The perpetrators can be relentless, charismatic and without conscience. I have seen some that appeal to my religious proclivity and some who claim to try to be helping a grandchild or friend who has lost his money in a foreign country and needs some money to get home. Do not fall for any of this! There are ways to check them out. Do it.

There are romantic approaches, distress approaches and "I am here to help you" approaches. No matter how much you are in need, do not get snookered. In my book, "Shams, Scams and Schemes" I shared several personal experiences with scams and how I have dealt with the perps. Perhaps it might give you some ideas.

12) **Beware of debit-card-addiction.** With this topic being well covered in a previous chapter, not much can be added here. Just know that unfettered debit card usage can be dangerous to your financial well-being. It is a major cause of people being deeply lost in the Financial Forest. Being both lost *and* embarrassed frequently go with debit-card-addiction.

13) **Track your daily expenditures.** Tracking your daily expenses is an effective treatment method for any personal finance malady. Especially helpful in relation to the debit card and credit card addiction is the *tracking your daily expenses* treatment. Just like tracking your out-of-pocket cash spending, tracking your debit and credit card spending will be of immense value to you. It will work to bring your over-all spending under control, and is part of the preparation of your personal budget.

14) **You are in the electronic age, make use of it.** If you use a mobile phone, a computer or electronic tablet, you have most of the resources needed to accomplish your budgeting dilemmas. Budget templates are found all over the place in word processing and spreadsheet applications. One of the most unique and helpful apps for your phone will even tract your debit card spending!

15) **Money does grow on trees.** If you are in the lumber business or in the logging business, those trees mean money for you. Assuredly, it makes little difference where you are employed; wherever you work, that is *your* income tree. So, in keeping with the metaphoric theme of this book, the trees can be both your wonderful friends or they can be your scariest archenemy.

Money must be utilized
Money must be managed
Money must be controlled
Money must be understood
Money must be a good friend

RETIRING GRACEFULLY

The word "retirement" is a very enticing word to most people, especially those who are below the age of about fifty. To them, the word "retirement" conjures up thoughts of travel to exotic places, spending time on the ski slopes and lounging on the beaches of Hawaii. And that is as it should be. But it must be financially planned for, actively pursued and methodically executed.

When the magic age of retirement approaches, however, a sort of paralytic fear begins to set in. Thoughts change a bit; our minds shift to the realities of health in our senior years, the probability of a reduction in buying power and the inevitability of death.

Questions arise; questions that a few years earlier were not of any concern. How much money will it take to maintain our lifestyle? Will we need to reduce our spending? What will we eliminate? Will healthcare expenses obliterate our savings? What if our kids need some financial help, will we be able to be of assistance?

So the far-reaching conundrum is this: How much is enough? The answer is the same as one I proffered earlier, *"It depends."* Are you entering retirement overladen with debt? Is it debt that was not abolished during your working years, but could have been? Are your insurances as you would have them? Will I need to take a part-time job, or perhaps more importantly, will I be *able* to work if necessary?

My heart goes out to an older lady who works at a local market. I do not know her age but she is clearly in her "golden" years from an age standpoint. During the Texas summer heat and humidity she takes her turn in the parking lot retrieving shopping carts, bringing them back into the store. She works as hard as anyone in the market. I am certain she does not do this because she wants pocket change. Necessity can be a unforgiving taskmaster. I do not know her circumstance so my observation must close here with this statement, *I admire her stamina and diligence.*

On a brighter side, I know a man who had a plan. Following retirement from his many years of service in a municipal employment position, he took a job at a local big box store. There he worked for about three years in order to complete his plan. Prior to his city employment he had worked in a Social Security covered program but not long enough to fully qualify for the benefits.

When the opportunity for employment arose in his city, and in his chosen profession, he accepted the offer. His plan was to work to retirement for the local government, then return to a Social Security job long enough to qualify for those benefits. It was planned for, worked toward and completed as designed. With two pensions he is retired comfortably, he and his wife are traveling to foreign countries and satisfying life-long dreams. They have done it because they had a plan and they followed the plan.

There are some very basic principles that I believe should be planned for and adhered to when it comes to retirement. The principles might be labeled "The Doctrine of Dennis." This because I have gleaned insight on the topic through my own "double-retirements," and through assisting others as they enter that magical and mystical phase of life. In an upcoming associated Quick-Read book, my focus is entirely on how to retire gracefully.

The one Doctrine of Dennis that can appropriately be addressed in this book is this: "In your retirement, fixed and variable expenses should be accompanied by guaranteed income." Without first establishing a budget and understanding how personal finances function in your early years, it is extremely difficult to manage your money in your golden years.

If you do not already have your retirement plan in place, or if it needs a sanity check, now is the time to get with it. To state an old worn-out phrase, *"You are not getting any younger!"* So now is the time to begin, and in the next few paragraphs I will share some valuable pre-retirement financial steps with you. It will take a little effort on your part but it will be a very enlightening experience and a helpful exercise.

In order to get your retirement plan in place, you must start as early as possible. Right now is as early as possible, and you are as young as you are going to get. It is of prime importance that you know your current spending patterns. Earlier in this book we discussed budgets, being lost in the financial forest and bad spending habits.

Here, I will show you how to: **First: F**ind your current location in the forest. Do this by identifying exactly where you are now spending your money. **Second:** You will then know what direction you must travel to get out of the forest in the shortest amount of time. **Third:** You can identify where the financial scrub-brush is located, where the financial rainstorms are forming and where the wild boars are lurking. With this learning, you will be able to better prioritize your spending, increase your savings and pay yourself instead of forfeiting interest to the credit card companies.

In order to create a reasonable and workable budget, you must first understand your wants and needs versus your actual spending patterns.

The utilization of this book's unique companion digital planning workbook is encouraged. Its purpose is to give you a self-educated understanding of your current financial situation. With a number of single data-point entries you will create a report similar to the one below. (Except it will be your own personal spending report.) You may get your personal digital workbook by logging on to: dennisbcall.com. Simply locate the workbook picture and click "download." Give yourself the edge in graceful retirement while improving your current personal finances.

Your early years' financial discipline
Brings about your golden years' financial freedom

4 months of actual spending allocation by %			Month 1	Month 2	Month 3	Month 4	Average	# Months
0.00%	0.00	Cash Spend	0.00	0.00	0.00	0.00	0.00	4
1.63%	227.55	Restaurant/Fast food	47.35	38.20	75.00	67.00	56.89	4
1.33%	185.37	C-stores/gasoline	40.30	57.80	49.00	38.27	46.34	4
0.13%	18.00	Banking	6.00	6.00	6.00	0.00	4.50	4
3.24%	452.36	Big Box & Department Store	108.46	236.90	39.00	68.00	113.09	4
5.87%	819.30	Grocery stores	207.00	254.30	158.00	200.00	204.83	4
1.00%	140.00	Entertainment	35.00	35.00	35.00	35.00	35.00	4
1.24%	172.40	Online stores	31.00	57.00	39.40	45.00	43.10	4
10.32%	1,440.00	Donations	360.00	360.00	360.00	360.00	360.00	4
4.69%	654.00	Auto expense	156.00	156.00	186.00	156.00	163.50	4
58.50%	8,165.00	Home and Utilities	2,355.00	1,900.00	1,980.00	1,930.00	2,041.25	4
1.22%	170.00	Personal Care	20.00	20.00	90.00	40.00	42.50	4
1.40%	195.00	Healthcare	40.00	40.00	80.00	35.00	48.75	4
1.12%	156.00	Personal	39.00	39.00	39.00	39.00	39.00	4
7.62%	1,064.00	Consumer loans	266.00	266.00	266.00	266.00	266.00	4
0.71%	99.00	Travel	99.00	0.00	0.00	0.00	24.75	4
#DIV/0!	31.00	Miscellaneous	28.00	0.00	0.00	0.00	7.75	4
100.00%	13,957.98						13,988.98	3,497.25	4

Deposits	
Jan-00	3,500.00
Jan-00	3,500.00
Jan-00	3,500.00
Jan-00	3,500.00
Total	14,000.00

Expenses paid out	13,988.98
Income/deposits	14,000.00
Surplus/Shortage	11.02

ABOUT THE AUTHOR

Dennis Boyd Call grew up an Idaho farm boy in the small town of Rigby, raising cattle and harvesting spuds. He met the love of his life while in high school and married Connie Wheeler shortly after graduation. Together they enjoyed 63 years of glorious marriage which produced 3 daughters, 3 sons and 25 grandchildren. Their posterity, which at the time of this writing includes 33 great grandchildren, have brought great joy to Dennis and Connie. Connie has been greatly missed since her passing in 2016.

Professionally, Dennis spent twenty-three years in swimming pool construction, eleven years in sales and sales management, and more than twenty years in the financial services business.

Now retired, Dennis has become a prolific writer and is publishing a series of Quick-Read books, including his series of "Books of Tens."

On the following page is a listing of the Quick-Read books written by Dennis Boyd Call.

Other Quick-Read books by Dennis Boyd Call:

"What?!? Another Meeting?"
"Finding Beauty in Desolation"
"Shams, Scams and Schemes"
"Traditionally Speaking …"
"Off by Just One"
"The Client Files"
"If You only Understood and if You Really Cared"
"Thoughts From a Spud Field"
"The Three-Cornered Blanket."
                    (co-authored with Denalee C. Chapman)

Books of Tens by Dennis Boyd Call:
"Ten Reasons Why I Swear"
"Ten Tips for a Happy Marriage"
"Ten P's of Sales Professionalism"
"Ten Tips for Raising a Family"
"Ten Reasons Why I Lie"
"Stand Up! Speak Up! Shut Up!"
"Leading From the Front"

dennisbcall.com

www.ingramcontent.com/pod-product-compliance
Lightning Source LLC
Chambersburg PA
CBHW072245170526
45158CB00003BA/1007